SPELLING
WEEKLY PRACTICE

4th Grade

This Book Belongs to

_____

_____

_____

Copyright©

About This book

This is a spelling weekly practice book for 4th grade with over 360 spelling words including games and activities to improve vocabulary and reading skills. This book is organized in a progressive skill-building way for kids to develop confidence in learning.

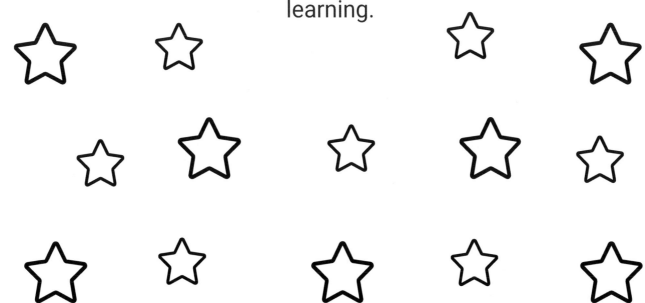

Week 1

build	fourth	cottage	tuba	loyal
tool	near	prize	nothing	gone

Trace

build
fourth
cottage
tuba
loyal
tool
near
prize
prize
gone

Write

Write

Circle the Correct Spelling

near	naer	nera	nare
tolo	tool	tloo	ootl
prize	prezi	przie	preiz

Word Scramble

Scramble the letters to spell the words correctly

uilbd   ☐☐☐☐☐   oolt   ☐☐☐☐

urthfo   ☐☐☐☐☐☐   nera   ☐☐☐☐

agecott   ☐☐☐☐☐☐☐   zepri   ☐☐☐☐☐

ubta   ☐☐☐☐   ingnoth   ☐☐☐☐☐☐☐

yallo   ☐☐☐☐☐   onge   ☐☐☐☐

Word Search

Find and circle the words below.

b	u	i	l	d	s	e	k	e
f	o	u	r	t	h	r	w	o
c	o	t	t	a	g	e	r	e
t	u	b	a	l	o	y	a	l
t	o	o	l	y	n	e	a	r
p	r	i	z	e	a	y	g	s
n	o	t	h	i	n	g	r	e
z	v	l	r	b	k	m	s	l
l	o	y	a	l	g	o	n	e

build
fourth
cottage
tuba
loyal
tool
near
prize
nothing
gone

Week 2

listen	field	return	until	circus
knight	passed	guard	teacher	choice

Trace

listen
field
return
until
circus
knight
passed
guard
teacher
choice

Write

Write

Circle the Correct Spelling

guard	gaurd	gurad	guadr
unlit	until	utiln	tilun
field	feild	filed	fidel

Word Scramble

Scramble the letters to spell the words correctly

tenlis

eldfi

urnret

tilun

cuscir

ightkn

sedpas

ardgu

hertec

icecho

Word Search

Find and circle the words below.

t	g	p	k	c	u	r	f	l
e	u	a	n	i	n	e	i	i
a	a	s	i	r	t	t	e	s
c	r	s	g	c	i	u	l	t
h	d	e	h	u	l	r	d	e
e	n	d	t	s	a	n	g	n
r	g	f	l	i	g	h	t	c
z	v	e	a	r	t	h	s	h
c	h	o	i	c	e	b	l	e

listen
field
return
until
circus
knight
passed
guard
teacher
choice

Week 3

deliver	hungry	forty	internet	sneeze
camera	middle	draw	threw	bubble

Trace

deliver
hungry
forty
internet
sneeze
camera
middle
draw
threw
bubble

Write

Write

Circle the Correct Spelling

cemara	camera	cemare	ceamra
draw	darw	drwa	darw
bbbelu	bebblu	bublbe	bubble

8

Word Scramble

Scramble the letters to spell the words correctly

verdeli ☐☐☐☐☐☐☐

gryhun ☐☐☐☐☐☐

tyfor ☐☐☐☐☐

eeezsn ☐☐☐☐☐☐

netinter ☐☐☐☐☐☐☐☐

ddlemi ☐☐☐☐☐☐

eracam ☐☐☐☐☐☐

drwa ☐☐☐☐

rewth ☐☐☐☐☐

bblebu ☐☐☐☐☐☐

Word Search

Find and circle the words below.

b	t	m	c	s	i	f	h	d
u	h	i	a	n	n	o	u	e
b	r	d	m	e	t	r	n	l
b	e	d	e	e	e	t	g	i
l	w	l	r	z	r	y	r	v
e	n	e	a	e	n	y	y	e
r	e	p	r	t	e	t	i	r
d	r	a	w	r	t	h	s	h
a	g	r	w	r	i	v	e	r

deliver
hungry
forty
internet
sneeze
camera
middle
draw
threw
bubble

scare	during	however	America	point
uncle	thumb	dislike	attack	instead

Trace

scare
during
however
America
point
uncle
thumb
dislike
attack
instead

Write

Write

Circle the Correct Spelling

thumb	thmub	thbum	thmub
unelc	uncle	uncel	unecl
point	ponit	piont	pinot

Word Scramble

Scramble the letters to spell the words correctly

arecs ⬜⬜⬜⬜⬜   cleun ⬜⬜⬜⬜⬜

ringud ⬜⬜⬜⬜⬜⬜   thbum ⬜⬜⬜⬜⬜

everhow ⬜⬜⬜⬜⬜⬜⬜   likedis ⬜⬜⬜⬜⬜⬜⬜

icaAmre ⬜⬜⬜⬜⬜⬜⬜   acktta ⬜⬜⬜⬜⬜⬜

intpo ⬜⬜⬜⬜⬜   eadinst ⬜⬜⬜⬜⬜⬜⬜

Word Search

Find and circle the words below.

s	c	a	r	e	s	e	k	i
d	u	r	i	n	g	u	n	n
h	o	w	e	v	e	r	r	s
A	m	e	r	i	c	a	o	t
p	o	i	n	t	l	u	n	e
u	n	c	l	e	i	n	g	a
t	h	u	m	b	g	h	t	d
d	i	s	l	i	k	e	k	t
a	t	t	a	c	k	b	l	e

scare
during
however
America
point
uncle
thumb
dislike
attack
instead

11

enough	buy	sentence	useful	change
once	know	blanket	yourself	writing

Trace

enough
buy
sentence
useful
change
once
know
blanket
yourself
writing

Write

Write

Circle the Correct Spelling

once	onec	ocen	oecn
chenga	change	chaneg	change
know	konw	kwno	kwon

Word Scramble

Scramble the letters to spell the words correctly

ugheno ☐☐☐☐☐☐   ceon ☐☐☐☐

uyb ☐☐☐   owkn ☐☐☐☐

angech ☐☐☐☐☐☐   ketanlb ☐☐☐☐☐☐☐

fuluse ☐☐☐☐☐☐   tingwri ☐☐☐☐☐☐☐

tencesen ☐☐☐☐☐☐   selfuroy ☐☐☐☐☐☐☐☐
                      ☐☐   ☐

Word Search

Find and circle the words below.

w	u	y	b	o	c	u	s	e
r	e	o	l	n	h	s	e	n
i	a	u	a	c	a	e	n	o
t	k	r	n	e	n	f	t	u
i	e	s	k	y	g	u	e	g
n	s	e	e	k	e	l	n	h
g	o	l	t	n	w	e	c	b
h	u	f	t	o	o	v	e	u
t	e	n	s	w	h	i	g	y

enough
buy
sentence
useful
change
once
know
blanket
yourself
writing

13

Week 6

against	wrist	written	battle	turtle
caring	jaw	alley	add	front

Trace

against
wrist
written
battle
turtle
caring
jaw
alley
add
front

Write

Write

Circle the Correct Spelling

front	fornt	fnort	front
alely	alley	aelly	aeyll
turtle	tutrle	turtel	teltur

Word Scramble

Scramble the letters to spell the words correctly

agstain ⬜⬜⬜⬜⬜⬜⬜   ingcar ⬜⬜⬜⬜⬜⬜

istwr ⬜⬜⬜⬜⬜   ajw ⬜⬜⬜

ttenwri ⬜⬜⬜⬜⬜⬜⬜   eylla ⬜⬜⬜⬜⬜

ttleab ⬜⬜⬜⬜⬜⬜   dad ⬜⬜⬜

tletur ⬜⬜⬜⬜⬜⬜   ontfr ⬜⬜⬜⬜⬜

Word Search

Find and circle the words below.

r	f	l	a	c	t	b	w	w	a
m	r	s	l	a	u	a	r	r	g
m	o	l	l	r	r	t	i	i	a
y	n	n	e	i	t	t	t	s	i
a	t	r	y	n	l	l	t	t	n
r	t	w	a	g	e	e	e	s	s
d	o	f	a	o	w	e	n	j	t
z	v	l	d	b	k	m	j	a	w
t	h	i	d	k	i	n	g	w	r

against
wrist
written
battle
turtle
caring
jaw
alley
add
front

15

Week 7

fruit	evening	angry	order	short
bottom	isn't	tuna	I'll	twice

Trace

fruit
evening
angry
order
short
bottom
isn't
tuna
I'll
twice

Write

Write

Circle the Correct Spelling

tuna	tnua	taun	atun
boottm	bottom	bototm	ttmboo
short	shrot	shtor	ortsh

Word Scramble

Scramble the letters to spell the words correctly

uitfr ☐☐☐☐☐

ningeev ☐☐☐☐☐☐☐

gryan ☐☐☐☐☐

deror ☐☐☐☐☐

ortsh ☐☐☐☐☐

boottm ☐☐☐☐☐☐

i'snt ☐☐☐☐☐

antu ☐☐☐☐

il'l ☐☐☐☐

icetw ☐☐☐☐☐

Word Search

Find and circle the words below.

h	i'	i	b	s	o	a	e	f
e	l	s	o	h	r	n	v	r
l	l	n'	t	o	d	g	e	u
t	d	t	t	r	e	r	n	i
w	e	e	o	t	r	y	i	t
i	s	t	m	d	s	y	n	s
c	o	u	l	o	w	e	g	e
e	v	n	r	b	k	m	s	l
t	a	a	h	o	m	e	y	f

fruit
evening
angry
order
short
bottom
isn't
tuna
I'll
twice

| carried | ground | dairy | sidewalk | curl |
| nobody | really | paper | mountain | raise |

Trace

carried
ground
dairy
sidewalk
curl
nobody
really
paper
mountain
raise

Write

Write

Circle the Correct Spelling

draiy	dariy	dairy	driay
ground	gronud	grunod	gruond
raise	rasie	riase	raeis

Word Scramble

Scramble the letters to spell the words correctly

llyear ☐☐☐☐☐☐

rlcu ☐☐☐☐

iedcarr ☐☐☐☐☐☐☐

bodyno ☐☐☐☐☐☐

undgro ☐☐☐☐☐☐

ppaer ☐☐☐☐☐

iryda ☐☐☐☐☐

isera ☐☐☐☐☐

walkdesi ☐☐☐☐☐☐☐☐

tainmoun ☐☐☐☐☐☐☐☐

Word Search

Find and circle the words below.

c	a	r	r	i	e	d	s	m
g	r	o	u	n	d	r	w	o
d	a	i	r	y	e	o	r	u
s	i	d	e	w	a	l	k	n
c	u	r	l	a	n	t	n	t
n	o	b	o	d	y	y	g	a
r	e	a	l	l	y	e	r	i
p	a	p	e	r	a	n	d	n
r	a	i	s	e	n	g	y	f

carried
ground
dairy
sidewalk
curl
nobody
really
paper
mountain
raise

Week 9

forgive	shown	caught	crumb	weather
ridge	mistake	dollar	zipper	yell

Trace

forgive
shown
caught
crumb
weather
ridge
mistake
dollar
zipper
yell

Write

Write

Circle the Correct Spelling

doallr	dollar	dlloar	doallr
mistake	misteka	miseatk	msitake
zipper	zipepr	zierpp	pperzi

Word Scramble

Scramble the letters to spell the words correctly

elly ☐☐☐☐

dgeri  ☐☐☐☐☐

wnsho ☐☐☐☐☐

takemis ☐☐☐☐☐☐☐

ghtcau ☐☐☐☐☐☐

llarod ☐☐☐☐☐☐

mbcru ☐☐☐☐☐

perpiz ☐☐☐☐☐☐

therwea ☐☐☐☐☐☐☐
☐

givefor ☐☐☐☐☐☐☐

Word Search

Find and circle the words below.

z	d	m	r	w	t	c	s	f
i	o	i	i	e	c	a	h	o
p	l	s	d	a	r	u	o	r
p	l	t	g	t	u	g	w	g
e	a	a	e	h	m	h	n	i
r	r	k	n	e	b	t	g	v
k	o	e	l	r	e	e	r	e
z	v	l	r	b	r	m	s	l
y	e	l	l	i	n	g	y	f

forgive
shown
caught
crumb
weather
ridge
mistake
dollar
zipper
yell

Week 10

engine	whether	happened	special	told
wonder	false	sixty	study	square

Trace

engine
whether
happened
special
told
wonder
false
sixty
study
square

Write

Write

Circle the Correct Spelling

special	spceial	speaicl	spaleci
fales	false	felsa	lsefa
study	sdytu	stuyd	sutdy

Word Scramble

Scramble the letters to spell the words correctly

gineen ☐☐☐☐☐☐   derwon ☐☐☐☐☐☐

therwhe ☐☐☐☐☐☐☐   lsefa ☐☐☐☐☐

cialpse ☐☐☐☐☐☐☐   xtysi ☐☐☐☐☐

oldt ☐☐☐☐   udyst ☐☐☐☐☐

enedhapp ☐☐☐☐☐☐   aresqu ☐☐☐☐☐☐
☐☐

Word Search

Find and circle the words below.

s	s	f	w	t	s	h	w	e
t	i	a	o	o	p	a	h	n
u	x	l	n	l	e	p	e	g
d	t	s	d	d	c	p	t	i
y	y	e	e	a	i	e	h	n
g	g	s	r	r	a	n	e	e
k	a	f	l	o	l	e	r	f
z	i	l	r	b	k	d	s	a
s	q	u	a	r	e	g	y	r

engine
whether
happened
special
told
wonder
false
sixty
study
square

23

Week 11

Saturday	center	became	goodbye	hiking
jacket	wood	chance	tired	heavy

Trace

Saturday
center
became
goodbye
hiking
jacket
wood
chance
tired
heavy

Write

Write

Circle the Correct Spelling

heavy	haevy	hvaey	hveay
jeakct	jaekct	jcaket	jacket
chance	chanec	chenac	chanca

Word Scramble

Scramble the letters to spell the words correctly

tercen

camebe

inghik

ketjca

dayursat

oowd

ancehc

redit

avyhe

byyoogd

Word Search

Find and circle the words below.

s	a	t	u	r	d	a	y	e
c	e	n	t	e	r	r	w	o
b	e	c	a	m	e	e	l	t
g	o	o	d	b	y	e	y	h
h	i	k	i	n	g	u	n	e
j	a	c	k	e	t	y	g	a
w	o	o	d	c	a	u	s	v
c	h	a	n	c	e	v	e	y
t	i	r	e	d	c	g	y	f

Saturday
center
became
goodbye
hiking
jacket
wood
chance
tired
heavy

25

Week 12

become	quiet	reason	company	whenever
young	united	office	full	answer

Trace

become

quiet

reason

company

whenever

young

united

office

full

answer

Write

Write

Circle the Correct Spelling

offiec	office	oficef	oiceff
yonug	yunog	young	yuong
company	campony	cmopany	cmapony

Word Scramble

Scramble the letters to spell the words correctly

mebeco ☐☐☐☐☐☐

ungyo ☐☐☐☐☐

ietqu ☐☐☐☐☐

teduni ☐☐☐☐☐☐

sonrea ☐☐☐☐☐☐

iceoff ☐☐☐☐☐☐

anypcom ☐☐☐☐☐☐☐

lluf ☐☐☐☐

everwhen ☐☐☐☐☐☐☐☐

werans ☐☐☐☐☐☐

Word Search

Find and circle the words below.

b	e	c	a	m	e	n	e	e
q	u	i	e	t	e	r	w	o
r	e	a	s	o	n	g	e	e
c	o	m	p	a	n	y	o	f
w	h	e	n	e	v	e	r	u
y	o	u	n	g	a	y	h	l
u	n	i	t	e	d	e	e	l
o	f	f	i	c	e	m	r	l
a	n	s	w	e	r	g	y	f

become
quiet
reason
company
whenever
young
united
office
full
answer

number	its	blood	giant	learn
picture	forever	board	glance	swimming

Trace

number
its
blood
giant
learn
picture
forever
board
glance
swimming

Write

Write

Circle the Correct Spelling

pictrue	pictuer	picture	turepic
forveer	forever	forvree	feevor
board	baord	boadr	borad

Word Scramble

Scramble the letters to spell the words correctly

bernum   ☐☐☐☐☐☐

sit   ☐☐☐

oodbl   ☐☐☐☐☐

antig   ☐☐☐☐☐

arnle   ☐☐☐☐☐

turepic   ☐☐☐☐☐☐☐

everfor   ☐☐☐☐☐☐☐

ardbo   ☐☐☐☐☐

ancegl   ☐☐☐☐☐☐

ingswimm   ☐☐☐☐☐☐ ☐☐

Word Search

Find and circle the words below.

n	u	m	b	e	r	e	k	s
i	t	s	d	a	y	r	w	w
b	l	o	o	d	t	l	e	i
g	i	a	n	t	e	b	o	m
l	e	a	r	n	g	h	t	m
p	i	c	t	u	r	e	n	i
f	o	r	e	v	e	r	e	n
b	o	a	r	d	k	m	s	g
g	l	a	n	c	e	g	y	f

number
its
blood
giant
learn
picture
forever
board
glance
swimming

Week 14

easier	alarm	picnic	simple	down
visit	wait	breakfast	certain	Indian

Trace

easier
alarm
picnic
simple
down
visit
wait
breakfast
certain
Indian

Write

Write

Circle the Correct Spelling

splemi	smiple	simpel	simple
indian	indain	ininda	indin
dnwo	dwon	down	dnow

Word Scramble

Scramble the letters to spell the words correctly

sierea ☐☐☐☐☐☐

armal ☐☐☐☐☐

nicpic ☐☐☐☐☐☐

plesim ☐☐☐☐☐☐

wndo ☐☐☐☐

sitvi ☐☐☐☐☐

itwa ☐☐☐☐

taincer ☐☐☐☐☐☐☐

dianin ☐☐☐☐☐☐

fastbreak ☐☐☐☐☐☐☐☐☐ ☐☐☐

Word Search

Find and circle the words below.

e	a	p	s	d	v	w	c	i
a	l	i	i	o	i	a	e	n
s	a	c	m	w	s	i	r	d
i	r	n	p	n	i	t	t	i
e	m	i	l	y	t	u	a	a
r	i	c	e	d	a	y	i	n
f	e	e	l	i	n	g	n	g
o	p	e	n	b	k	m	s	l
b	r	e	a	k	f	a	s	t

easier
alarm
picnic
simple
down
visit
wait
breakfast
certain
Indian

31

Week 15

holiday	alone	beggar	copy	village
space	choose	word	worse	important

Trace

holiday
alone
beggar
copy
village
space
choose
word
worse
important

Write

Write

Circle the Correct Spelling

alone	aleno	aleon	leona
speca	space	speac	eacsp
rodw	wrod	word	wodr

Word Scramble

Scramble the letters to spell the words correctly

dayholi ⬚⬚⬚⬚⬚⬚⬚   acespa ⬚⬚⬚⬚⬚⬚

leona ⬚⬚⬚⬚⬚   seooch ⬚⬚⬚⬚⬚⬚

ggarbe ⬚⬚⬚⬚⬚⬚   rdow ⬚⬚⬚⬚

pyco ⬚⬚⬚⬚   rsewo ⬚⬚⬚⬚⬚

agevill ⬚⬚⬚⬚⬚⬚⬚   tantporim ⬚⬚⬚⬚⬚⬚⬚⬚⬚

Word Search

Find and circle the words below.

h	a	b	c	v	s	c	w	b
o	l	e	o	i	p	h	o	w
l	o	g	p	l	a	o	r	o
i	n	g	y	l	c	o	d	r
d	e	a	e	a	e	s	e	s
a	y	r	n	g	a	e	s	e
y	o	f	l	e	w	e	r	e
w	o	n	'	t	k	m	s	l
i	m	p	o	r	t	a	n	t

holiday
alone
beggar
copy
village
space
choose
word
worse
important

33

Week 16

oh	oil	honey	thirty	question
metal	groceries	fifth	person	almost

Trace

oh
oil
honey
thirty
question
metal
groceries
fifth
person
almost

Write

Write

Circle the Correct Spelling

thirty	thrity	tthiry	ttyhir
porsen	person	prosen	porsne
honey	henoy	hoeny	hoyne

Word Scramble

Scramble the letters to spell the words correctly

ho   ☐☐

ilo   ☐☐☐

neyho   ☐☐☐☐☐

rtythi   ☐☐☐☐☐☐

tionques   ☐☐☐☐☐☐☐☐

talme   ☐☐☐☐☐

fthfi   ☐☐☐☐☐

sonper   ☐☐☐☐☐☐

mostal   ☐☐☐☐☐☐

riesgroce   ☐☐☐☐☐☐☐☐☐

Word Search

Find and circle the words below.

o	h	t	w	e	e	e	o	i	l
h	o	n	e	y	k	e	p	t
t	h	i	r	t	y	g	r	e
q	u	e	s	t	i	o	n	m
m	e	t	a	l	e	u	n	y
g	r	o	c	e	r	i	e	s
f	i	f	t	h	w	e	r	e
k	p	e	r	s	o	n	s	l
t	a	l	m	o	s	t	n	g

oh
oil
honey
thirty
question
metal
groceries
fifth
person
almost

libraries	father	second	afraid	we'll
finish	sharp	sound	railroad	tube

Trace

libraries
father
second
afraid
we'll
finish
sharp
sound
railroad
tube

Write

Write

Circle the Correct Spelling

sound	suond	sunod	sodun
sharp	shrap	shpra	shapr
tebu	tube	betu	beut

Word Scramble

Scramble the letters to spell the words correctly

therfa ☐☐☐☐☐☐

shfini ☐☐☐☐☐☐

ondsec ☐☐☐☐☐☐

rapsh ☐☐☐☐☐

raidaf ☐☐☐☐☐☐

undso ☐☐☐☐☐

llw'e ☐☐☐☐☐

betu ☐☐☐☐

riesralib ☐☐☐☐☐☐
☐☐☐

roadrail ☐☐☐☐☐☐☐
☐☐

Word Search

Find and circle the words below.

r	s	s	f	w	a	s	f	l
a	o	h	i	e	f	e	a	i
i	u	a	n	l	r	c	t	b
l	n	r	i	l	a	o	h	r
r	d	p	s	m	i	n	e	a
o	s	u	h	d	d	d	r	r
a	o	f	l	o	w	n	r	i
d	o	m	m	u	n	i	t	e
a	d	v	t	u	b	e	g	s

libraries
father
second
afraid
we'll
finish
sharp
sound
railroad
tube

Week 18

couch	quite	useless	sure	knew
country	kneel	zebra	wouldn't	garden

Trace

couch
quite
useless
sure
knew
country
kneel
zebra
wouldn't
garden

Write

Write

Circle the Correct Spelling

country	cuontry	cunotry	counytr
gerdan	garden	dengar	dengra
zeabr	zerba	zabre	zebra

Word Scramble

Scramble the letters to spell the words correctly

uchco ☐☐☐☐☐

trycoun ☐☐☐☐☐☐☐

itequ ☐☐☐☐☐

neelk ☐☐☐☐☐

lessuse ☐☐☐☐☐☐☐

braze ☐☐☐☐☐

resu ☐☐☐☐

dengar ☐☐☐☐☐☐

newk ☐☐☐☐

uldwont ☐☐☐☐☐☐☐

Word Search

Find and circle the words below.

g	a	r	d	e	n	d	a	y
w	o	u	l	d	n	t	w	s
z	e	b	r	a	f	o	r	o
k	n	e	e	l	r	b	o	u
c	o	u	n	t	r	y	t	t
s	u	r	e	k	n	e	w	h
u	s	e	l	e	s	s	w	e
q	u	i	t	e	o	p	s	l
c	o	u	c	h	r	a	i	d

couch

quite

useless

sure

knew

country

kneel

zebra

wouldn't

garden

Week 19

though	you're	cardboard	true	eighth
invite	juice	grew	rough	twenty

Trace

though
you're
cardboard
true
eighth
invite
juice
grew
rough
twenty

Write

Write

Circle the Correct Spelling

invite	inivte	iinvte	inevit
tewnty	twenty	twnety	twtney
gwre	gwer	gerw	grew

Word Scramble

Scramble the letters to spell the words correctly

oughth ☐☐☐☐☐☐

reyou ☐☐☐☐☐

uetr ☐☐☐☐

htheig ☐☐☐☐☐☐

boardcard ☐☐☐☐☐☐☐☐☐

vitein ☐☐☐☐☐☐

iceju ☐☐☐☐☐

rewg ☐☐☐☐

ughro ☐☐☐☐☐

entytw ☐☐☐☐☐☐

Word Search

Find and circle the words below.

r	g	j	i	e	t	c	y	t
o	r	u	n	i	r	a	o	h
u	e	i	v	g	u	r	u	o
g	w	c	i	h	e	d	r	u
h	o	e	t	t	g	b	e	g
s	m	o	e	h	a	o	g	h
l	e	n	g	t	h	a	r	e
t	e	n	t	h	k	r	s	l
t	w	e	n	t	y	d	e	r

though
you're
cardboard
true
eighth
invite
juice
grew
rough
twenty

41

Week 20

neither	women	sixth	pretty	trouble
seen	hour	whose	excuse	meant

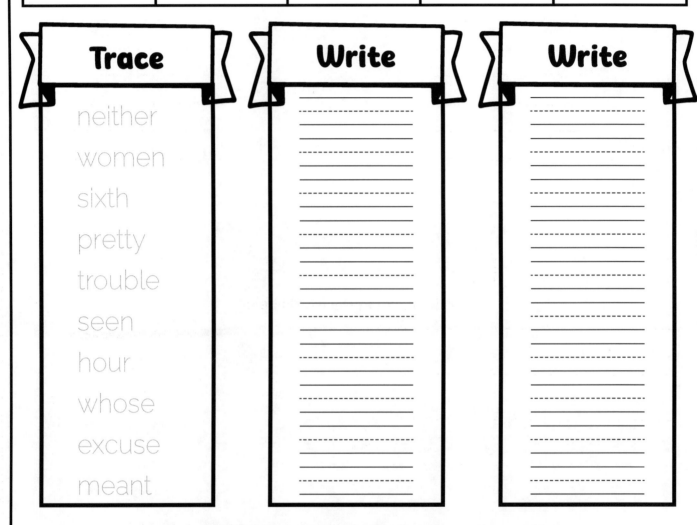

Trace

neither
women
sixth
pretty
trouble
seen
hour
whose
excuse
meant

Write

Write

Circle the Correct Spelling

hour	huor	hruo	hrou
sene	seen	snee	eens
meant	maent	antme	antem

Word Scramble

Scramble the letters to spell the words correctly

thernei ⬜⬜⬜⬜⬜⬜⬜

menwo ⬜⬜⬜⬜⬜

xthsi ⬜⬜⬜⬜⬜

ettypr ⬜⬜⬜⬜⬜⬜

ubletro ⬜⬜⬜⬜⬜⬜⬜

eesn ⬜⬜⬜⬜

urho ⬜⬜⬜⬜

osewh ⬜⬜⬜⬜⬜

cuseex ⬜⬜⬜⬜⬜⬜

antme ⬜⬜⬜⬜⬜

Word Search

Find and circle the words below.

n	e	i	t	h	e	r	r	e
w	o	m	e	n	y	r	w	o
s	i	x	t	h	t	o	r	e
p	r	e	t	t	y	b	o	m
t	r	o	u	b	l	e	n	y
s	e	e	n	d	h	o	u	r
w	h	o	s	e	w	e	r	e
e	x	c	u	s	e	l	a	w
m	e	a	n	t	s	e	i	f

neither
women
sixth
pretty
trouble
seen
hour
whose
excuse
meant

43

Week 21

across	breath	mailbox	steel	group
medal	drain	danger	animal	haven't

Trace

across
breath
mailbox
steel
group
medal
drain
danger
animal
haven't

Write

Write

Circle the Correct Spelling

animal	aminal	amnial	animle
gruop	group	gorup	gopru
steel	seetl	stlee	leest

44

Word Scramble

Scramble the letters to spell the words correctly

rossac ☐☐☐☐☐☐

eathbr ☐☐☐☐☐☐

boxmail ☐☐☐☐☐☐☐

teels ☐☐☐☐☐

oupgr ☐☐☐☐☐

dalme ☐☐☐☐☐

aindr ☐☐☐☐☐

gerdan ☐☐☐☐☐☐

malani ☐☐☐☐☐☐

ven'tha ☐☐☐☐☐☐

Word Search

Find and circle the words below.

a	d	d	m	g	s	m	b	a
n	a	r	e	r	t	a	r	c
i	n	a	d	o	e	i	e	r
m	g	i	a	u	e	l	a	o
a	e	n	l	p	l	b	t	s
l	r	u	l	d	a	o	h	s
d	o	f	t	w	h	x	t	e
z	v	l	r	b	k	m	s	l
r	h	a	v	e	n	t	p	f

across
breath
mailbox
steel
group
medal
drain
danger
animal
haven't

early	strange	else	famous	state
follow	building	garden	people	clothes

Trace

early
strange
else
famous
state
follow
building
garden
people
clothes

Write

Write

Circle the Correct Spelling

garden	dengar	gardne	graden
lyear	early	eraly	lyrea
follow	fololw	ollofw	flloow

Word Scramble

Scramble the letters to spell the words correctly

arlye ☐☐☐☐☐

angestr ☐☐☐☐☐☐☐

seel ☐☐☐☐

ousfam ☐☐☐☐☐☐

atets ☐☐☐☐☐

llowof ☐☐☐☐☐☐

thesclo ☐☐☐☐☐☐☐

dengar ☐☐☐☐☐☐

plepeo ☐☐☐☐☐☐

dingbuil ☐☐☐☐☐☐☐☐

Word Search

Find and circle the words below.

e	s	e	f	s	f	b	g	p
a	t	l	a	t	o	u	a	e
r	r	s	m	a	l	i	r	o
l	a	e	o	t	l	l	d	p
y	n	r	u	e	o	d	e	l
k	g	a	s	d	w	i	n	e
e	e	b	s	t	a	n	e	n
t	h	l	r	s	t	g	t	g
c	l	o	t	h	e	s	y	f

early
strange
else
famous
state
follow
building
garden
people
clothes

Week 23

choose	either	doesn't	tried	captain
style	library	sudden	earth	their

Trace

choose
either
doesn't
tried
captain
style
library
sudden
earth
their

Write

Write

Circle the Correct Spelling

their	thire	thier	thrie
style	sytle	lesty	sytel
tried	tired	tidre	tiedr

Word Scramble

Scramble the letters to spell the words correctly

oosech ☐☐☐☐☐☐

ylest ☐☐☐☐☐

therie ☐☐☐☐☐☐

rarylib ☐☐☐☐☐☐☐

esn'tdo ☐☐☐☐☐☐

ddensu ☐☐☐☐☐☐

iedtr ☐☐☐☐☐

eirth ☐☐☐☐☐

taincap ☐☐☐☐☐☐
☐

earth ☐☐☐☐☐

Word Search

Find and circle the words below.

e	s	l	s	c	t	d	e	c
a	u	i	t	a	i	o	i	h
r	d	b	y	p	r	e	t	o
t	d	r	l	t	e	s	h	o
h	e	a	e	a	d	n'	e	s
d	n	r	n	i	a	t	r	e
k	o	y	o	n	s	e	r	e
z	v	l	r	b	k	m	s	l
k	i	t	h	e	i	r	e	r

choose
either
doesn't
tried
captain
style
library
sudden
earth
their

Week 24

weight	gasoline	large	search	city
reach	alphabet	cheer	judge	peaceful

Trace

weight
gasoline
large
search
city
reach
alphabet
cheer
judge
peaceful

Write

Write

Circle the Correct Spelling

judge	jduge	jedgu	dguje
raech	reach	chrea	chera
city	ctiy	ityc	itcy

Word Scramble

Scramble the letters to spell the words correctly

ghtwei ☐☐☐☐☐☐   achre ☐☐☐☐☐

tyci ☐☐☐☐   phabetal ☐☐☐☐☐☐☐☐

argel ☐☐☐☐☐   eerch ☐☐☐☐☐

rchsea ☐☐☐☐☐☐   dgeju ☐☐☐☐☐

linegaso ☐☐☐☐☐☐☐☐   fulpeace ☐☐☐☐☐☐☐☐

Word Search

Find and circle the words below.

w	e	i	g	h	t	e	k	j
g	a	s	o	l	i	n	e	u
l	a	r	g	e	y	m	r	d
s	e	a	r	c	h	s	t	g
c	i	t	y	y	e	u	n	e
r	e	a	c	h	a	y	g	s
a	l	p	h	a	b	e	t	e
c	h	e	e	r	p	f	u	l
p	e	a	c	e	f	u	l	h

weight
gasoline
large
search
city
reach
alphabet
cheer
judge
peaceful

51

Week 25

discover	moment	earth	sleeve	ruler
eighty	plane	happiest	enjoy	monkey

Trace

discover
moment
earth
sleeve
ruler
eighty
plane
enjoy
happiest
monkey

Write

Write

Circle the Correct Spelling

monkey	menkoy	mnokey	mnekoy
plena	plane	plean	eanpl
enjyo	enjoy	eonjy	enoyj

Word Scramble

Scramble the letters to spell the words correctly

mentmo ☐☐☐☐☐☐

rthea ☐☐☐☐☐

eeevsl ☐☐☐☐☐☐

lerru ☐☐☐☐☐

coverdis ☐☐☐☐☐☐☐☐

htyeig ☐☐☐☐☐☐

kenchic ☐☐☐☐☐☐☐

joyen ☐☐☐☐☐

keymon ☐☐☐☐☐☐

ppiestha ☐☐☐☐☐☐☐☐

Word Search

Find and circle the words below.

m	h	c	e	r	s	e	m	d
o	a	h	i	u	l	a	o	i
n	p	i	g	l	e	r	m	s
k	p	c	h	e	e	t	e	c
e	i	k	t	r	v	h	n	o
y	e	e	y	u	e	y	t	v
s	s	n	l	t	w	e	r	e
t	t	l	r	b	k	m	s	r
t	a	l	e	n	j	o	y	f

discover
moment
earth
sleeve
ruler
eighty
chicken
happiest
enjoy
monkey

roof	beauty	minute	around	third
toward	tennis	slowly	better	chief

Trace

roof
beauty
minute
around
third
toward
tennis
slowly
better
chief

Write

Write

Circle the Correct Spelling

bettre	better	beettr	breett
third	thrid	tirdh	tdhir
around	arundo	rounda	daroun

Word Scramble

Scramble the letters to spell the words correctly

oofr ☐☐☐☐

wardto ☐☐☐☐☐☐

utybea ☐☐☐☐☐☐

nniste ☐☐☐☐☐☐

nutemi ☐☐☐☐☐☐

wlyslo ☐☐☐☐☐☐

undaro ☐☐☐☐☐☐

tterbe ☐☐☐☐☐☐

irdth ☐☐☐☐☐

iefch ☐☐☐☐☐

Word Search

Find and circle the words below.

r	o	o	f	e	v	e	n	e
b	m	a	t	t	t	s	b	c
e	i	r	h	o	e	l	e	h
a	n	o	i	w	n	o	t	i
u	u	u	r	a	n	w	t	e
t	t	n	d	r	i	l	e	f
y	e	d	l	d	s	y	r	e
z	v	l	r	b	k	m	s	l
t	a	l	b	r	e	a	d	f

roof
beauty
minute
around
third
toward
tennis
slowly
better
chief

Week 27

turn	remember	zoo	button	degree
example	pencil	suit	stories	divide

Trace

turn

remember

zoo

button

degree

example

pencil

suit

stories

divide

Write

Write

Circle the Correct Spelling

divide	diivde	dviide	dviied
pcneil	pencil	pnecil	cilpen
siut	suit	stiu	stui

Word Scramble

Scramble the letters to spell the words correctly

rntu ☐☐☐☐

ozo ☐☐☐

onttbu ☐☐☐☐☐☐

reedeg ☐☐☐☐☐☐

memberre ☐☐☐☐☐☐☐☐

pleexam ☐☐☐☐☐☐☐

cilpen ☐☐☐☐☐☐

itsu ☐☐☐☐

idediv ☐☐☐☐☐☐

riessto ☐☐☐☐☐☐☐

Word Search

Find and circle the words below.

s	d	s	p	e	d	b	r	t
t	i	u	e	x	e	u	e	u
o	v	i	n	a	g	t	m	r
r	i	t	c	m	r	t	e	n
i	d	u	i	p	e	o	m	y
e	e	s	l	l	e	n	b	z
s	o	t	e	e	m	e	e	o
e	v	w	r	i	t	e	r	o
t	a	l	k	i	d	o	e	s

turn
remember
zoo
button
degree
example
pencil
suit
divide
stories

ninth	cover	kitchen	bridge	answer
peanut	cough	season	quilt	lonely

Trace

ninth
cover
kitchen
bridge
answer
peanut
cough
season
quilt
lonely

Write

Write

Circle the Correct Spelling

cough	cuogh	cuohg	couhg
saeson	season	sonsea	snosea
lonely	lenoly	nelylo	nelyol

Word Scramble

Scramble the letters to spell the words correctly

nthni ▢▢▢▢▢

anutpe ▢▢▢▢▢▢

verco ▢▢▢▢▢

ughco ▢▢▢▢▢

chenkit ▢▢▢▢▢▢▢

sonsea ▢▢▢▢▢▢

dgebri ▢▢▢▢▢▢

iltqu ▢▢▢▢▢

werans ▢▢▢▢▢▢

nelylo ▢▢▢▢▢▢

Word Search

Find and circle the words below.

q	s	c	p	a	b	k	c	n
u	e	o	e	n	r	i	o	i
i	a	u	a	s	i	t	v	n
l	s	g	n	w	d	c	e	t
t	o	h	u	e	g	h	r	h
t	n	u	t	r	e	e	g	i
k	i	f	i	s	n	n	t	m
z	n	l	r	b	b	l	u	e
l	o	n	e	l	y	g	y	f

ninth
cover
kitchen
bridge
answer
peanut
cough
season
quilt
lonely

street	decide	above	earlier	grown
everybody	known	agree	sauce	gentle

Trace

street
decide
above
earlier
grown
everybody
known
agree
sauce
gentle

Write

Write

Circle the Correct Spelling

agree	ageer	argee	eearg
knnow	known	nowkn	knwon
gentle	tlegen	telgen	gnetel

Word Scramble

Scramble the letters to spell the words correctly

reetst ☐☐☐☐☐☐   knonw ☐☐☐☐☐

cidede ☐☐☐☐☐☐   greea ☐☐☐☐☐

oveab ☐☐☐☐☐   ucesa ☐☐☐☐☐

owngr ☐☐☐☐☐   tlegen ☐☐☐☐☐☐

lierear ☐☐☐☐☐☐☐   bodyevery ☐☐☐☐☐☐☐☐☐
☐☐

Word Search

Find and circle the words below.

s	t	r	e	e	t	t	e	g
d	e	c	i	d	e	a	r	e
a	b	o	v	e	f	o	r	n
e	a	r	l	i	e	r	r	t
g	r	o	w	n	r	n	n	l
k	n	o	w	n	a	y	g	e
a	g	r	e	e	w	e	r	e
s	a	u	c	e	k	m	s	l
e	v	e	r	y	b	o	d	y

street
decide
above
earlier
grown
everybody
known
agree
sauce
gentle

brought	radio	banana	idea	mother
tomorrow	done	whole	pleasing	think

Trace

brought
radio
banana
idea
mother
tomorrow
done
whole
pleasing
think

Write

Write

Circle the Correct Spelling

dark	drak	dkra	dkar
sprot	sport	sptor	sptro
right	rigth	rgiht	ightr

Word Scramble

Scramble the letters to spell the words correctly

ughtbro ☐☐☐☐☐☐☐

diora ☐☐☐☐☐

nanaba ☐☐☐☐☐☐

deai ☐☐☐☐

singplea ☐☐☐☐☐☐☐☐

node ☐☐☐☐

olewh ☐☐☐☐☐

inkth ☐☐☐☐☐

thermo ☐☐☐☐☐☐

morrowto ☐☐☐☐☐☐☐☐

Word Search

Find and circle the words below.

b	r	o	u	g	h	t	n	t
r	a	d	i	o	e	r	w	o
b	a	n	a	n	a	o	r	m
i	d	e	a	e	a	t	o	o
m	o	t	h	e	r	t	a	r
d	o	n	e	d	a	y	i	r
w	h	o	l	e	w	e	r	o
t	h	i	n	k	i	g	h	w
p	l	e	a	s	i	n	g	f

brought
radio
banana
idea
mother
tomorrow
done
whole
pleasing
think

63

Week 31

it's	holiday	another	drawer	zero
towel	town	since	police	children

Trace

it's
holiday
another
drawer
zero
towel
town
since
police
children

Write

Write

Circle the Correct Spelling

another	anethor	therano	threano
police	poliec	poilce	piolce
since	snice	sncie	sncei

64

Word Scramble

Scramble the letters to spell the words correctly

st'i ☐☐☐

dayholi ☐☐☐☐☐☐☐

therano ☐☐☐☐☐☐☐

werdra ☐☐☐☐☐☐

roze ☐☐☐☐

welto ☐☐☐☐☐

wnto ☐☐☐☐

inces ☐☐☐☐☐

licepo ☐☐☐☐☐☐

drenchil ☐☐☐☐☐☐☐☐

Word Search

Find and circle the words below.

i	h	a	d	z	t	t	s	p
t'	o	n	r	e	o	o	i	o
s	l	o	a	r	w	w	n	l
e	i	t	w	o	e	n	c	i
c	d	h	e	n	l	a	e	c
u	a	e	r	s	m	i	l	e
r	y	r	l	b	a	d	g	e
e	n	l	r	b	k	m	s	l
c	h	i	l	d	r	e	n	f

it's
holiday
another
drawer
zero
towel
town
since
police
children

movement	hurry	found	often	different
built	nickel	student	howl	they're

Trace

movement
hurry
found
often
different
built
nickel
student
howl
they're

Write

Write

Circle the Correct Spelling

built	bulit	butli	tlubi
fuond	found	fnoud	fondu
hurry	huyrr	rryhu	rryuh

Word Scramble

Scramble the letters to spell the words correctly

urryh □□□□□

dentstu □□□□□□□

undfo □□□□□

wlho □□□□

tenof □□□□□

ey'reth □□□□□□

iltbu □□□□□

kelnic □□□□□□

erentdiff □□□□□□□□□

mentmove □□□□□□□□

Word Search

Find and circle the words below.

m	o	v	e	m	e	n	t	d
h	f	o	b	n	s	h	t	i
u	o	f	u	i	t	o	h	f
r	u	t	i	c	u	w	e	f
r	n	e	l	k	d	l	y'	e
y	d	n	t	e	e	p	r	r
d	z	f	l	l	n	e	e	e
a	e	l	r	b	t	m	y	n
r	e	w	r	i	t	e	y	t

movement
hurry
found
often
different
built
nickel
student
howl
they're

Week 33

crayon	wrote	machine	double	awhile
scrap	roast	together	common	broken

Trace

crayon
wrote
machine
double
awhile
scrap
roast
together
common
broken

Write

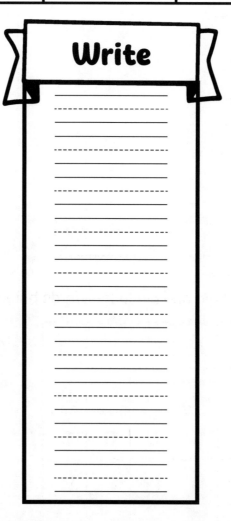

Write

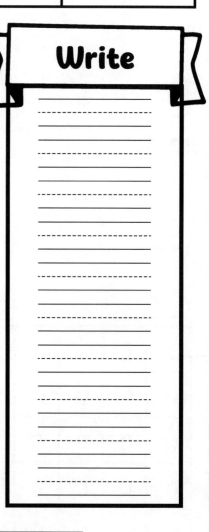

Circle the Correct Spelling

common	comnom	mmonco	moncom
brekon	broken	kenbro	knebro
roast	raost	astro	astor

68

Word Scramble

Scramble the letters to spell the words correctly

yoncra ☐☐☐☐☐☐

otewr ☐☐☐☐☐

chinema ☐☐☐☐☐☐☐

ubledo ☐☐☐☐☐☐

whilea ☐☐☐☐☐☐

rapsc ☐☐☐☐☐

astro ☐☐☐☐☐

kenbro ☐☐☐☐☐☐

mmonco ☐☐☐☐☐☐

getherto ☐☐☐☐☐☐☐☐

Word Search

Find and circle the words below.

c	t	r	s	a	d	m	w	c
o	o	o	c	w	o	a	r	r
m	g	a	r	h	u	c	o	a
m	e	s	a	i	b	h	t	y
o	t	t	p	l	l	i	e	o
n	h	e	e	e	e	n	l	n
k	e	f	l	o	w	e	r	e
z	r	l	m	o	n	t	h	l
b	r	o	k	e	n	g	y	f

crayon
wrote
machine
double
awhile
scrap
roast
together
common
broken

Week 34

head	charge	chore	mirror	doctor
place	heard	shout	faint	seventy

Trace

head
charge
chore
mirror
doctor
place
heard
shout
faint
seventy

Write

Write

Circle the Correct Spelling

faint	fiant	faitn	fiatn
place	plaec	paecl	lacep
heard	haerd	harde	dhear

Word Scramble

Scramble the letters to spell the words correctly

eadh ☐☐☐☐

acepl ☐☐☐☐☐

argech ☐☐☐☐☐☐

ardhe ☐☐☐☐☐

orech ☐☐☐☐☐

outsh ☐☐☐☐☐

rrormi ☐☐☐☐☐☐

intfa ☐☐☐☐☐

tordoc ☐☐☐☐☐☐

ventyse ☐☐☐☐☐☐☐

Word Search

Find and circle the words below.

f	s	h	p	d	m	c	c	h
a	h	e	l	o	i	h	h	e
i	o	a	a	c	r	o	a	a
n	u	r	c	t	r	r	r	d
t	t	d	e	o	o	e	g	y
g	m	i	n	r	r	y	e	s
k	t	r	a	d	e	e	r	e
z	f	r	e	e	k	m	s	l
s	e	v	e	n	t	y	y	f

head
charge
chore
mirror
doctor
place
heard
shout
faint
seventy

Week 35

studied	except	truly	few	couldn't
ocean	parent	hospital	paste	suppose

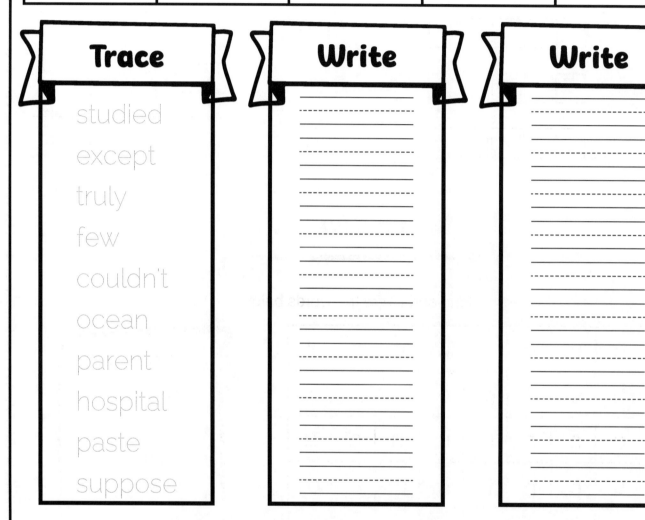

Trace

studied
except
truly
few
couldn't
ocean
parent
hospital
paste
suppose

Write

Write

Circle the Correct Spelling

paste	pesta	paset	setpa
parent	rentpa	rentap	entrpa
truly	turly	rulyt	lytru

Word Scramble

Scramble the letters to spell the words correctly

diedstu ☐☐☐☐☐☐☐

eanoc ☐☐☐☐☐

xcepte ☐☐☐☐☐☐

entpar ☐☐☐☐☐☐

rulyt ☐☐☐☐☐

pitalhos ☐☐☐☐☐☐☐☐

ewf ☐☐☐

astep ☐☐☐☐☐

ouldn'tc ☐☐☐☐☐☐☐

posesup ☐☐☐☐☐☐☐

Word Search

Find and circle the words below.

s	p	h	p	c	f	t	e	s
u	a	o	a	o	e	r	x	t
p	s	s	r	u	w	u	c	u
p	t	p	e	l	h	l	e	d
o	e	i	n	d	e	y	p	i
s	l	t	t	n'	r	i	t	e
e	a	a	l	t	w	e	r	d
z	n	l	r	b	k	m	s	l
o	c	e	a	n	e	a	l	f

studied

except

truly

few

couldn't

ocean

parent

hospital

paste

suppose

Week 36

neighbor	easy	laugh	world	dawn
electric	bounce	no one	music	work

Trace

neighbor
easy
laugh
world
dawn
electric
bounce
no one
music
work

Write

Write

Circle the Correct Spelling

music	mcsiu	sicmu	muisc
easy	esay	asye	syea
laugh	luagh	lauhg	ghlau

Word Scramble

Scramble the letters to spell the words correctly

asye □□□□

oneno □□□□□

ughla □□□□□

sicmu □□□□□

orldw □□□□□

rkow □□□□

wnda □□□□

uncebo □□□□□□

tricele □□□□□□□
□

ghbornei □□□□□□□
□□

Word Search

Find and circle the words below.

n	e	a	s	y	o	r	b	e
e	l	a	u	g	h	o	n	e
i	w	o	r	l	d	o	r	g
g	d	a	w	n	r	b	o	l
h	b	o	u	n	c	e	n	a
b	n	o	o	n	e	y	g	s
o	m	u	s	i	c	e	r	s
r	w	o	r	k	k	m	u	g
e	l	e	c	t	r	i	c	f

neighbor
easy
laugh
world
dawn
electric
bounce
no one
music
work

Word search solution week 1

```
b u i l d s e k e
f o u r t h r w o
c o t t a g e r e
t u b a l o y a l
t o o l y n e a r
p r i z e a y g s
n o t h i n g r e
z v l r b k m s l
l o y a l g o n e
```

Word search solution week 2

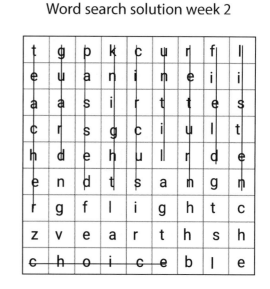

```
t g p k c u r f l
e u a n i n e i i
a a s i r t t e s
c r s g c i u l t
h d e h u l r d e
e n d t s a n g n
r g f l i g h t c
z v e a r t h s h
c h o i c e b l e
```

Word search solution week 3

```
b t m c s i f h d
u h i a n n o u e
b r d m e t r n l
b e d e e t g i
l w l r z r y r v
e n e a e n y y e
r e p r t e i r
d r a w r t h s h
a g r w r i v e r
```

Word search solution week 4

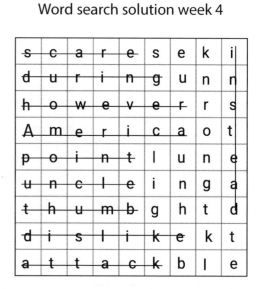

```
s c a r e s e k i
d u r i n g u n n
h o w e v e r r s
A m e r i c a o t
p o i n t l u n e
u n c l e i n g a
t h u m b g h t d
d i s l i k e k t
a t t a c k b l e
```

Word search solution week 5

```
w u y b o c u s e
r e o l n h s e n
i a u a c a e n o
t k r n e n f t u
i e s k y g u e g
n s e e k e l n h
g o l t n w e c b
h u f t o o v e u
t e n s w h i g y
```

Word search solution week 6

```
r f l a c t b w w a
m r s l a u a r r g
m o l r r t i i a
y n e i t t s i
a t r y n l l t n
r t w a g e e s s
d o f a o w e n j t
z v l d b k m j a w
t h i d k i n g w r
```

Word search solution week 7

h	i'	i	b	s	o	a	e	f
e	l	s	o	h	r	m	v	r
l	l	n'	t	o	d	g	e	u
t	d	t	t	r	e	r	n	i
w	e	e	o	t	r	y	i	t
i	i	s	t	m	d	s	y	n	s
c	o	u	l	o	w	e	g	e
e	v	n	r	b	k	m	s	l
t	a	a	h	o	m	e	y	f

Word search solution week 8

c	a	r	r	i	e	d	s	m
g	r	o	u	n	d	r	w	o
d	a	i	r	y	e	o	r	u
s	i	d	e	w	a	l	k	n
c	u	r	l	a	n	t	n	t
n	o	b	o	d	y	y	g	a
r	e	a	l	l	y	e	r	i
p	a	p	e	r	a	n	d	n
r	a	i	s	e	n	g	y	f

Word search solution week 9

z	d	m	r	w	t	c	s	f
i	o	i	e	c	a	h	o
p	l	s	d	a	r	u	o	r
p	l	t	g	t	u	g	w	g
e	a	a	e	h	m	h	n	i
r	r	k	n	e	b	t	g	v
k	o	e	l	r	e	e	r	e
z	v	l	r	b	r	m	s	l
y	e	l	l	i	n	g	y	f

Word search solution week 10

s	s	f	w	t	s	h	w	e
t	i	a	o	o	p	a	h	n
u	x	l	n	e	p	e	g
d	t	s	d	d	c	p	t	i
y	y	e	e	a	i	e	h	n
g	g	s	r	a	n	e	e
k	a	f	l	o	l	e	r	f
z	i	l	r	b	k	d	s	a
s	q	u	a	r	e	g	y	r

Word search solution week 11

s	a	t	u	r	d	a	y	e
c	e	n	t	e	r	r	w	o
b	e	c	a	m	e	e	l	t
g	o	o	d	b	y	e	y	h
h	i	k	i	n	g	u	n	e
j	a	c	k	e	t	y	g	a
w	o	o	d	c	a	u	s	v
c	h	a	n	c	e	v	e	y
t	i	r	e	d	c	g	y	f

Word search solution week 12

b	e	c	a	m	e	n	e	e
q	u	i	e	t	e	r	w	o
r	e	a	s	o	n	g	e	e
c	o	m	p	a	n	y	o	f
w	h	e	n	e	v	e	r	u
y	o	u	n	g	a	y	h	l
u	n	i	t	e	d	e	e	l
o	f	f	i	c	e	m	r	l
a	n	s	w	e	r	g	y	f

Word search solution week 13

n	u	m	b	e	r	e	k	s
i	t	s	d	a	y	r	w	w
b	l	o	o	d	t	l	e	i
g	i	a	n	t	e	b	o	m
l	e	a	r	n	g	h	t	m
p	i	c	t	u	r	e	n	i
f	o	r	e	v	e	r	e	n
b	o	a	r	d	k	m	s	g
g	l	a	n	c	e	g	y	f

Word search solution week 14

e	a	p	s	d	y	w	c	i
a	l	i	i	o	a	e	n	
s	a	c	m	w	s	i	r	d
i	r	n	p	n	i	t	t	i
e	m	i	l	y	t	u	a	a
r	i	c	e	d	a	y	i	n
f	e	e	l	i	n	g	n	g
o	p	e	n	b	k	m	s	l
b	r	e	a	k	f	a	s	t

Word search solution week 15

h	a	b	c	y	s	c	w	b
o	l	e	o	i	p	h	d	w
l	o	g	p	l	a	o	r	o
i	n	y	l	c	o	d	r	
d	e	a	e	a	s	e	s	
a	y	n	n	g	a	e	s	e
y	o	f	l	e	w	e	r	e
w	o	n	'	t	k	m	s	l
i	m	p	o	r	t	a	n	t

Word search solution week 16

o	h	t	w	e	e	o	i	l
h	o	n	e	y	k	e	p	t
t	h	i	r	t	y	g	r	e
q	u	e	s	t	i	o	n	m
m	e	t	a	l	e	u	n	y
g	r	o	c	e	r	i	e	s
f	i	f	t	h	w	e	r	e
k	p	e	r	s	o	n	s	l
t	a	l	m	o	s	t	n	g

Word search solution week 17

r	s	s	f	w	a	s	f	l
a	o	h	i	e	f	e	a	i
i	u	a	n	l	r	c	t	b
l	n	r	i	l	a	o	h	r
r	d	p	s	m	i	n	e	a
o	s	u	h	d	d	d	r	r
a	o	f	l	o	w	n	r	i
d	o	m	m	u	n	i	t	e
a	d	v	t	u	b	e	g	s

Word search solution week 18

g	a	r	d	e	n	d	a	y
w	o	u	l	d	n	t	w	s
z	e	b	r	a	f	o	r	o
k	n	e	e	l	r	b	o	u
c	o	u	n	t	r	y	t	t
s	u	r	e	k	n	e	w	h
u	s	e	l	e	s	s	w	e
q	u	i	t	e	o	p	s	l
c	o	u	c	h	r	a	i	d

Word search solution week 19

r	g	j	i	e	t	c	y	t
o	r	u	n	i	r	a	o	h
u	e	i	v	g	u	r	u	o
g	w	c	i	h	e	d	r	u
h	o	e	t	g	b	e	g	
s	m	o	e	h	a	o	g	h
l	e	n	g	t	h	a	r	e
t	e	n	t	h	k	r	s	l
t	w	e	n	t	y	d	e	r

Word search solution week 20

n	e	i	t	h	e	r	r	e
w	o	m	e	n	y	r	w	o
s	i	x	t	h	t	o	r	e
p	r	e	t	t	y	b	o	m
t	r	o	u	b	l	e	n	y
s	e	e	n	d	h	o	u	r
w	h	o	s	e	w	e	r	e
e	x	c	u	s	e	l	a	w
m	e	a	n	t	s	e	i	f

Word search solution week 21

a	d	d	m	g	s	m	b	a
n	a	r	e	r	t	a	r	c
i	n	a	d	o	e	i	e	r
m	g	i	a	u	e	l	a	o
a	e	h	l	p	l	b	t	s
l	r	u	l	d	a	o	h	s
d	o	f	t	w	h	x	t	e
z	v	l	r	b	k	m	s	l
r	h	a	v	e	n	t	p	f

Word search solution week 22

e	s	e	f	s	f	b	g	p
a	t	l	a	t	o	u	a	e
r	r	s	m	a	l	i	r	o
l	a	e	o	t	l	l	d	p
y	n	r	u	e	o	d	e	l
k	g	a	s	d	w	i	n	e
e	e	b	s	t	a	n	e	n
t	h	l	r	s	t	g	t	g
c	l	o	t	h	e	s	y	f

Word search solution week 23

e	s	l	s	c	t	d	e	c
a	u	i	t	a	i	o	i	h
r	d	b	y	p	r	e	t	o
t	d	r	l	t	e	s	h	o
h	e	a	e	a	d	n'	e	s
d	m	r	n	i	a	t	r	e
k	o	y	o	n	s	e	r	e
z	v	l	r	b	k	m	s	l
k	i	t	h	e	i	r	e	r

Word search solution week 24

w	e	i	g	h	t	e	k	j
g	a	s	o	l	i	n	e	u
l	a	r	g	e	y	m	r	d
s	e	a	r	c	h	s	t	g
c	i	t	y	y	e	u	n	e
r	e	a	c	h	a	y	g	s
a	l	p	h	a	b	e	t	e
c	h	e	e	r	p	f	u	l
p	e	a	c	e	f	u	l	h

Word search solution week 25

m	h	c	e	r	s	e	m	d
o	a	h	i	u	l	a	o	i
n	p	i	g	l	e	r	m	s
k	p	c	h	e	e	t	e	c
e	i	k	t	r	v	h	n	o
y	e	e	y	u	e	y	t	v
s	s	m	l	t	w	e	r	e
t	t	l	r	b	k	m	s	r
t	a	l	e	n	j	o	y	f

Word search solution week 26

r	o	o	f	e	v	e	n	e
b	m	a	t	t	t	s	b	c
e	i	r	h	o	e	l	e	h
a	n	o	i	w	n	o	t	i
u	u	r	a	n	w	t	e	f
t	t	n	d	r	i	l	e	f
y	e	d	l	d	s	y	r	e
z	v	l	r	b	k	m	s	l
t	a	l	b	r	e	a	d	f

Word search solution week 27

s	d	s	p	e	d	b	r	t
t	i	u	e	x	e	u	e	u
o	v	i	n	a	g	t	m	r
r	i	t	c	m	r	t	e	n
i	d	u	i	p	e	o	m	y
e	e	s	l	l	e	n	b	z
s	o	t	e	e	m	e	e	o
e	v	w	r	i	t	e	r	o
t	a	l	k	i	d	o	e	s

Word search solution week 28

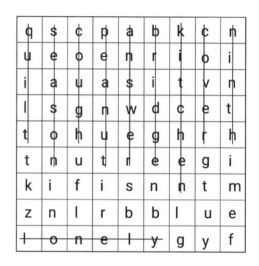

q	s	c	p	a	b	k	c	n
u	e	o	e	n	r	i	o	i
i	a	u	a	s	i	t	v	n
l	s	g	n	w	d	c	e	t
t	o	h	u	e	g	h	r	h
t	n	u	t	r	e	e	g	i
k	i	f	i	s	n	n	t	m
z	n	l	r	b	b	l	u	e
l	o	n	e	l	y	g	y	f

Word search solution week 29

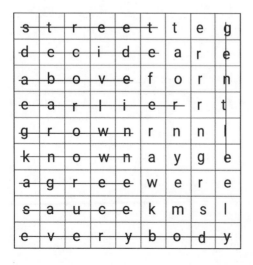

s	t	r	e	e	t	t	e	g
d	e	c	i	d	e	a	r	e
a	b	o	v	e	f	o	r	n
e	a	r	l	i	e	r	r	t
g	r	o	w	n	r	n	n	l
k	n	o	w	n	a	y	g	e
a	g	r	e	e	w	e	r	e
s	a	u	c	e	k	m	s	l
e	v	e	r	y	b	o	d	y

Word search solution week 30

b	r	o	u	g	h	t	n	t
r	a	d	i	o	e	r	w	o
b	a	n	a	n	a	o	r	m
i	d	e	a	e	a	t	o	o
m	o	t	h	e	r	t	a	r
d	o	n	e	d	a	y	i	r
w	h	o	l	e	w	e	r	o
t	h	i	n	k	i	g	h	w
p	l	e	a	s	i	n	g	f

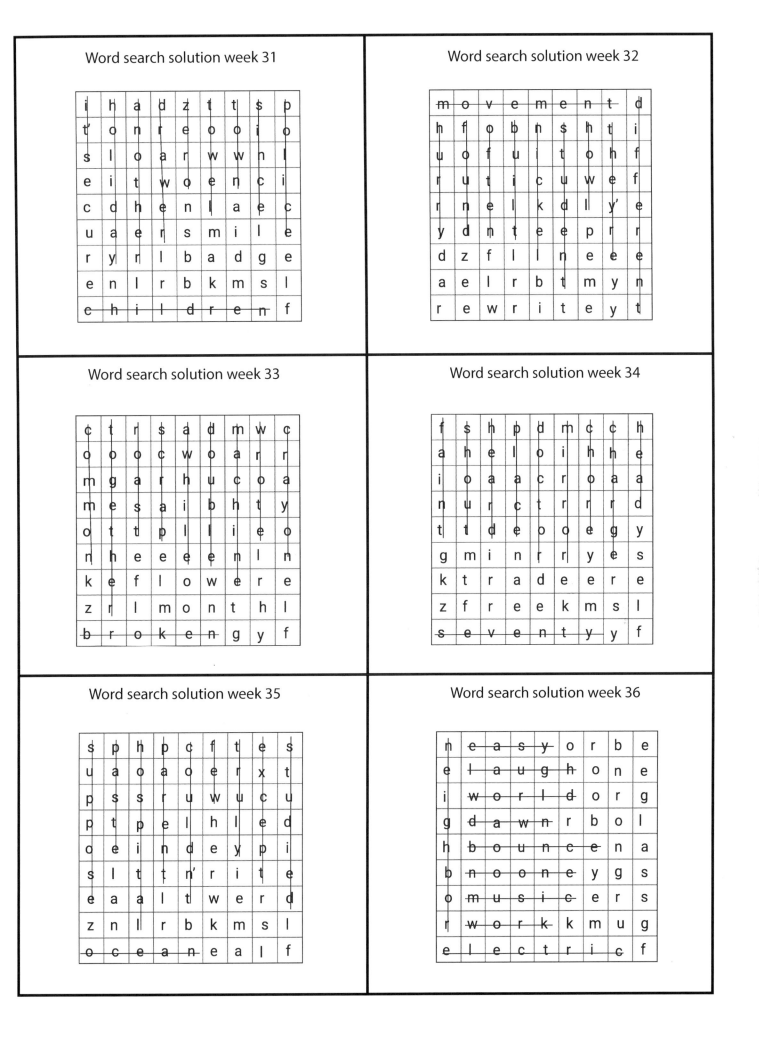

Word search solution week 31
Word search solution week 32
Word search solution week 33
Word search solution week 34
Word search solution week 35
Word search solution week 36

Made in United States
Troutdale, OR
02/05/2024

17464499R00046